KILLER WOMEN

Brenda Irish Heintzelman

~

KILLER WOMEN

Researching the cases included in this book of women who have killed their children, or their partner or ex-partner, has been interesting, to say the least. What I find most intriguing is that the case from 1977 of Francine Hughes, who was a battered woman long before society had a clue what the term even meant, was the one case in which it seems the defendant was treated most fairly by the justice system.

The year was 1977. The defendant lived in a rural area of Michigan, near the state capital, but oh so far away when one considers the zeitgeist of the times. In Dansville, Michigan in 1977 women knew their place. And abusive men knew that as long as they didn't kill their wife or children that anything less than murder would likely be considered a family matter, one which local law enforcement preferred to not get involved with.

Women in Dansville, Michigan in 1977 could call for help all they wanted. But the sad reality was that there was no help available for them to escape an abusive relationship.

The Violence Against Women and Children Act of 1994 (VAWA) would change all that. With the passage of VAWA, law enforcement was forced, by law, to care.

But Francine Hughes killed her abusive ex-husband long before VAWA. So why was her case handled so differently from all the rest? Because her lawyer, Arjen Greydanus, was clearly a man who cared about his client and her right to be treated with dignity.

Arjen Greydanus was a man before his time. And every new lawyer would do well to study this case in order to learn what empathy and compassion truly look like in the legal profession.

Francine Hughes was allowed to present the evidence of the abuses she suffered before she killed her abuser. She was allowed to present the evidence because her lawyer fought like hell for her right to speak of the atrocities she had endured. She was allowed to present the evidence because the court was also compassionate to the defendant and ensured that she received a fair trial.

Every defendant, of course, deserves the same benefit of having a lawyer who will fight like hell for their story to be told. But not every court allows it. And not every court ensures that the Battered Woman Syndrome defense isn't misused either.

Killer Women is an opinion essay written to explore the cases of twelve women who have killed either the man they claimed had abused them, or women who have killed their child(ren). By comparing and contrasting these cases, it is my hope that we can learn from these tragic incidents how to better help other women who may be dangerously close to committing murder.

~

For comparison sake, there are nine categories we will explore in KILLER WOMEN – Age, number of children, whether the killer was a victim of childhood abuse, socioeconomic status, whether the killer woman had any help available to her, education and employment options, stressors, infidelity, and how the killer presented herself post incident. By comparing these categories, it is my hope we can learn to identity the commonalities which may help us to become better prepared to help other woman who may be at risk of becoming a killer.

But first, here is a short summary of each case, including conviction and sentencing information, listed in order from the oldest to the most recent case.

~

FRANCINE HUGHES

Late in the evening on March 9, 1977, Francine Hughes, of Dansville, Michigan, poured gasoline under and all around the bed that her ex-husband was sleeping in, lit the match, and ran for her life. At trial, Hughes was found not guilty by reason of temporary insanity in one of the first cases involving the "battered-woman syndrome" as a defense. Francine's case was made famous by Farrah Fawcett in the movie "The Burning Bed".

~

DIANE DOWNS

Late at night on May 19, 1983, Diane Downs, of Cottage Grove, Oregon, told her three children that she was taking them for a drive. It was a school night and past their bedtime. She drove down a deserted country road in the dark, stopped her car, took a gun out of her trunk, and shot her children. Downs was convicted of both murder and attempted murder and sentenced to life in prison plus fifty years with the possibility of parole. Diane's case was made famous by Farrah Fawcett in the movie "Small Sacrifices".

~

BETTY BRODERICK

Early in the morning on November 5, 1989, Betty Broderick of San Diego, California, drove to her ex-husband's house, snuck into the master bedroom, and shot him. She ripped the phone line out of the wall and ran for her life. Broderick was convicted of 2nd degree murder and sentenced to 32 years to life in prison with the possibility of parole.

~

SUSAN SMITH

On October 25, 1994, Susan Smith of Union, South Carolina reported that her vehicle had been carjacked by a black man who drove away with her sons still inside. She later confessed that she let her car roll into a nearby lake with her two sons inside. Smith was convicted of two counts of murder and sentenced to life in prison with the possibility of parole.

~

DARLIE ROUTIER

On June 6, 1996, at 2:31 a.m. Darlie Routier, of Rowlett, Texas dialed 911 and reported that an intruder had stabbed her and two of her children. There was no intruder. Routier was convicted of capital murder and sent to death row.

~

ANDREA YATES

On June 20, 2001, shortly after her husband left for work, Andrea Yates, of Houston, Texas drowned her five children, one by one, then called her husband and told him that he needed to come home. Yates was found not guilty by reason of insanity.

~

SUSAN WRIGHT

Late one night on January 13, 2003, Susan Wright, of Houston, Texas stabbed her husband 193 times then buried his body in the backyard. Wright was convicted of murder and sentenced to serve 20 years in prison.

~

DARLENE GENTRY

Just after six a.m. on November 9, 2005, Darlene Gentry of Robinson, Texas, shot and killed her husband then staged the scene as if an intruder had killed him and stolen his guns. Gentry was convicted of murder and sentence to serve sixty years in prison with the possibility of parole.

~

MARY WINKLER

Early in the morning on March 22, 2006, Mary Winkler, of Selmer, Tennessee, shot her husband in the back with a 12-gauge shotgun as he lay sleeping in their bed. She ripped the phone line out of the wall then drove away with their children to go spend the day at the beach. Winkler was convicted of voluntary manslaughter and sentenced to serve 210 days in prison.

~

JODI ARIAS

Late one afternoon on June 4, 2008, Jodi Arias of Yreka, California brutally stabbed and shot her ex-boyfriend. Arias was convicted of murder and sentenced to life in prison without the possibility of parole.

~

SHAYNA HUBERS

On October 12, 2012, Shayna Hubers, a student at the University of Kentucky in Lexington, shot her ex-boyfriend in the face. Instead of immediately dialing 911, she called her mother to ask what she should say to the police. During her police interview, she laughed and said that she gave him the nose job he always wanted. Hubers was convicted of murder and sentenced to life in prison with the possibility of parole.

~

COLLEEN MCKERNAN

On December 31, 2013, Colleen McKernan, of Masillion, Ohio, dialed 911 and told the dispatcher that her husband had hit her for the last time. According to the coroner's testimony, her husband had been shot 10 times and he'd been shot in the face from less than two feet away. McKernan admitted to voluntary manslaughter and was sentenced to serve seven years in prison.

~

Nine Categories for Comparison

Age

Number of children

Whether the killer was a victim of childhood abuse

Socioeconomic status

Whether the killer had any help available to her

Education and employment options

Stressors

Infidelity

How the killer presented herself post incident

~

Age

Francine Hughes was thirty years old when she killed her abusive ex-husband, "Mickey" Hughes.

Diane Downs was twenty-eight years old when she murdered her daughter, Cheryl, and attempted to murder her daughter, Christie, and her son, Danny.

Betty Broderick was forty-two years old when she killed her abusive ex-husband, Daniel Broderick.

Susan Smith was twenty-three years old when she murdered her children, Michael and Alex.

Darlie Routier was twenty-six years old when she murdered her children, Devon and Damon.

Andrea Yates was thirty-seven years old when she killed her children – Noah, Mary, Luke, Paul, and John.

Susan Wright was twenty-seven years old when she murdered her husband, Jeff.

Darlene Gentry was thirty-one years old when she murdered her husband, Keith.

Mary Winkler was thirty-three years old when she murdered her husband, Matthew.

Jodi Arias was twenty-eight years old when she murdered her ex-boyfriend, Travis Alexander, at his home in Mesa, Arizona.

Shayna Hubers was twenty-one years old when she murdered her ex-boyfriend, Ryan Postin.

Colleen McKernan was twenty-six years old when she murdered her husband, Rob McKernan.

Summary of Category Number One

AGE

The youngest killer on our list for comparison is Shayna Hubers who killed her ex-boyfriend when she was just twenty-one years old. Her ex-boyfriend, Ryan Postin, was twenty-nine when she killed him. Shayna was in college when she dated Ryan. She was pursuing her master's degree in psychology, but of course at age twenty-one she had many years to go in school before she would have reached that goal. Ryan was a successful lawyer who came from a wealthy and very well-connected family.

According to Shayna, Ryan would often ridicule her for being backward, dense, and from a poor family background. In fact, Shayna was articulate, intelligent, and successful. But it's clear that she was not able to let go. Ryan was already dating other women and it appears he was using his young ex-girlfriend when it was convenient for him to do so. The night before the murder, Ryan even invited Shayna to his parents' home for a family dinner. And just one day later, he was demanding that she leave him alone. He was in a hurry to get her out of his condo because he had a date with another woman that evening and obviously having a twenty-one-year old ex-girlfriend in his condo simply wouldn't do.

Nobody deserves to be killed for simply trying to cut the relationship off. But it does appear that in this case the twenty-nine-year old lawyer was playing with fire.

This case is similar to the Jodi Arias case. Jodi and her ex-boyfriend were older than Shayna, of course, but the dynamics of the relationship were the same. Both men presented themselves to others as wanting to rid themselves of their ex-girlfriends. Yet, both men continued to use their ex-girlfriends when it was convenient or pleasurable for them to do so.

The message is clear – if a man is going to use a woman for sex, while simultaneously bashing her to his friends and family members, then it weakens the claim that the ex-girlfriend was stalking him or refusing to let him go.

Both Shayna Hubers and Jodi Arias clearly had issues going on that prevented them from being able to let go as long as the men they "loved" continued to use them in the bedroom.

Both men appeared to mistreat their ex-girlfriends. I realize that in both cases social media HATERS have chosen to believe that both men were pure as the driven snow. However, they both belittled and demeaned their ex-girlfriends so badly that it makes you wonder if perhaps both killers' claims that they were abused may be true after all.

At the time of their deaths, both men had plans to meet another woman. Ryan had a date that very night. Jodi's victim, Travis, had plans to go on vacation with another woman the following day.

~

The oldest killer in our comparison list is Betty Broderick who was almost forty-two years old when she killed her abusive ex-husband. She married him in 1969 and claims that on their wedding night he all but raped her. Nine months later their first baby was born. Betty suffered through miscarriages and the birth of her five children without any support from her husband. He was busy earning his law degree while Betty worked as an elementary school teacher to support the growing family.

Betty suffered the loss of one of her babies, a little boy, shortly after he was born.

Betty's husband was selfish, egotistical, and shallow. When she married him, he was completing his internship as an M.D. So, Betty thought she was marrying a doctor. However, after the wedding he announced she would have to keep working because he didn't want to be a doctor. He wanted to be a lawyer instead.

It was 1969 and Betty was raised in a strict Catholic home. So, divorce was simply not an option. She hung in there hoping for the day that she could realize her dream of becoming a stay-at-home mom. But when her husband finally did start supporting the family, Betty's dream turned into a nightmare when her husband started openly cheating on her with a twenty-two-year old woman who he put on the payroll at his law office.

The young woman couldn't even type. But that didn't seem to matter to her very married lover/boss. Betty endured five more years of abuse and embarrassment before the two divorced. But her abusive ex-husband would not leave her alone. She was tormented by both him and his mistress for years.

And finally, right before her forty-second birthday, Betty went to his house to commit suicide right in front of him if he refused to honor her final plea to just leave her the hell alone. She said that when she entered his bedroom that he lunged for the phone and the gun just went off.

Five times.

~

Betty Broderick was almost forty-two years old when she killed her abusive ex-husband and Andrea Yates was thirty-seven years old when she killed her five children. Both women became killers at ages or under circumstances which hormones may have played a huge role. Both women had multiple pregnancies. And Betty was old enough that she may have been entering perimenopause.

Both women viewed their primary role in life to be a mother to their children. Both women held strong religious beliefs and were raised in strict and very religious homes. Both women married men who shared their deep religious beliefs. In both cases, marriage to them was forever.

Both women were highly intelligent and well-educated. Andrea Yates was an R.N. and Betty Broderick was an elementary school teacher. Both women transitioned from being career women who worked full-time outside the home to being able to recognize their dreams of becoming a stay-at-home mom.

Both women were married to men who seemed to rule the roost while the women did as they were told and followed the lead of their husbands who were considered to be the head of their household.

Both women appeared to have a history of issues which would lead the casual observer to believe they would have both benefitted by receiving regular counseling with a mental health expert who was highly trained in issues such as identity, roles, and self-esteem.

Could it be that both women had been intellectually stifled for too long when they attempted to abide by the teachings of their childhoods which led them to want to be stay-at-home moms? Could it be that if both women had continued working full-time outside the home that they would not have suffered in the end?

~

On the other end of the spectrum, Shayna Hubers was just twenty-one years old and Susan Smith was just twenty-three years old. Both young women were suffering the break-up of a love relationship. Shayna shot and killed the man who had broken up with her. Susan drowned her two sons after the young man she had been dating broke it off because he didn't want to have children.

It appears in both of these cases that the killers were also guilty of social-climbing in their relationships and were perhaps incapable of accepting defeat in their mission to rise above their current status. Shayna wanted to be married to a lawyer, especially one who was from a wealthy and well-connected family. Susan's ex-boyfriend was the son of one of the owners of the company she worked for. Without him, she was a single-mom who was struggling financially. So, she evidently thought she would get her children out of her way in order to try to convince her ex-boyfriend that the two of them should be together after all.

~

We'll consider Broderick, Yates, Hubers, and Smith outliers for the purpose of this comparison in the age category. So, we have the majority of killer women in our comparison ranging in age from twenty-six to thirty-three years old.

Specifically, we have two at age twenty-six, Routier and McKernan, one at age twenty-seven, Wright, two at age twenty-nine, Arias and Downs, one at age thirty, Hughes, one at age thirty-one, Gentry, and one at age thirty-three, Winkler.

The two women at age twenty-six were Darlie Routier and Colleen McKernan. Darlie Routier murdered two of her children following an evening discussion with her husband which she would later describe in her written statement to the police as "we had words between us". In fact, the couple was in big trouble. Just one month before the murders Darlie had contemplated suicide. Her husband, Darin, would later say that he became angry with her for how she was feeling, and they never discussed it again. Darlie shared with her closest friend that she knew she needed help but that she thought it would look bad in a custody battle if she went for help. The couple was experiencing severe financial difficulties. They were behind in their house payments, their credit card payments, and the husband's shop rent too. They owed back taxes, their car was in need of repairs, and they had two big vacations planned but were turned down by the bank for a five-thousand-dollar loan. Darlie's husband, Darin Routier, should have taken his children to his parents' house and filed for custody because it seems that clearly the couple was on the verge of divorce and his wife was showing serious signs of instability. Instead, after they "had words" he went up to bed and left her and the children to sleep in the main floor family room. Just one and a half-hour later, after he went up to bed, two of his children were dead.

The same issue of impending divorce was probably true for the other twenty-six-year old, Colleen McKernan. Colleen was dubbed in the news as being "bride killa" because she murdered her husband when they were still newlyweds. But even though they weren't married for very long, it appears their marriage was a disaster from the start. They argued constantly and struggled with power and control as it seems Colleen expected to have total control over her seemingly conflict-averse husband.

Her husband, Rob McKernan, had a son from a previous marriage who did not want to have to be alone with Colleen. This was a serious issue in their marriage as Colleen believed that the problem was everybody was giving in to the boy's demands. However, the child was probably able to spot the mean streak in his step-mom and refused to be her victim.

The night that she killed her husband, the couple had just attended a new year's eve party that they were asked to leave because of Colleen's angry outburst when she suddenly exploded and started verbally abusing Rob at the top of her lungs.

As Rob was walking her to the car, she screamed out to their friends that none of what happened was her fault!

Probably when they got home her husband told her they were through. And within just minutes of them returning home, he was dead. When Colleen called the police she said that he had hit her for the last time.

What Rob should have done, of course, was not even get in the car with her at the party. He should have left the party and driven directly to his parents' home and filed for divorce as soon as the court opened along with a protection order to keep Colleen away from both him and his son.

At age twenty-seven, we have Susan Wright who killed her husband, Jeff Wright, after convincing him to allow her to tie him up to the bedposts for some wild fun in the bedroom. Susan stabbed Jeff one-hundred and ninety-three times, buried him in the backyard, then proceeded to worry that he would return and beat on her if the house wasn't clean.

I think that Susan Wright's claims that her husband was abusive were true. And the reason I believe her is in part because of her father-in-law's statements that he made against her.

One of her husband's ex-girlfriends appeared in court to substantiate Susan's claims that her husband was abusive. Both the witness and Susan had at some point in their lives worked as strippers. So, the father-in-law made some sort of crass remark about the "club of the strippers" coming together to support each other. He also called his daughter-in-law all sorts of nasty names when in fact, it appears likely that his son was abusive toward her.

Of course, being abusive toward his wife does not mean that he deserved to be tortured and killed. But his father's comments kind of makes you wonder if maybe Susan was in fact being abused not only by her husband but also belittled and demeaned by her husband's family too.

At age twenty-eight we have Arias and Downs. It's kind of fitting I think for Arias and Downs to be in the same group even if it's only based on their age at the time of their crimes. But of all of the women in this study, Arias and Downs really appear to have committed the most horrendous of crimes.

I'm not making excuses for the others or trying to say that the other crimes were not serious or painful for the victims' families to deal with. I'm simply saying that in the world of killer women that Arias and Downs both hold a certain distinction of being exceptionally evil.

Jodi Arias clearly planned to murder her ex-boyfriend. She bought gas cans and she traveled hundreds of miles to first have sex with her victim then to mutilate his body before running out the door to her next boyfriend's house a few states away.

Diane Downs also appears to have planned to murder her children when her very married ex-boyfriend told her that he didn't want to have kids.

Both women planned out to murder people they claimed to love. They both trapped their victims in such a way that there was no escape or chance of survival. And they both looked right into the camera after the murders and smiled.

They both seemed to thrive on the attention they received after the murders. They both used their fake voices to try to manipulate the male investigators, as if they were actually trying to flirt at times with the police officers and prosecutors.

Both women acted as if they were in total control of those around them. Both women were articulate and highly intelligent. But both women struggled to keep their stories straight.

At age thirty, we have Francine Hughes who, unlike Arias and Downs, garners sympathy from anybody who researches her case. Francine did everything she could possibly do to simply protect her children and defend herself from her abusive ex-husband. She begged for help from the police, from her parents, from social services, and from her abuser's parents too. And nobody helped her. There was no safe escape for Francine Hughes and her children. She was poor, dependent on social services, and she was enrolled in a vocational course to learn secretarial skills so she could try to get a job and provide for her children herself.

The night that she killed her abuser he had taken her books from the secretarial course she was enrolled in and torn them to shreds. Then he knocked her around the kitchen then raped her and when he was done he went to the kitchen, grabbed a beer, then returned to the bedroom to get a good night's sleep. He didn't live there. He lived right next door at his parents' house. But any time he wanted to beat on her then he just made himself at home.

At age thirty-one we have Darlene Gentry who was an accomplished nurse with a successful career who failed to offer any emergency medical help to her husband, Keith, after she shot him. Instead, Darlene staged the scene to appear as if an intruder had entered the home, shot her husband, and stolen his guns, all while she was in the shower getting ready for work.

At age thirty-three we have Mary Winkler who shot her minister husband in the back while he was sleeping with his 12-gauge shotgun. Mary did not work outside the home. Instead, she made the mistake of getting mixed up with some sort of fraudulent get-rich-quick scheme that ended up costing her about sixteen-thousand dollars. The bank was on to her and her gig was up. She and her husband were expected to meet with the bank within just hours of when she shot her husband.

After she killed her husband she put the shotgun in the back of her van where her children were waiting for her and she drove off to spend the day at the beach with her kids.

Here are the results of the age comparison specific to the entire group, including the outliers.

Mode – twenty-six and twenty-eight years old.

Median – twenty-eight years old.

Mean – twenty-nine years and four months old.

And, here are the results of the age comparison not including the outliers.

Mode – twenty-six and twenty-eight years old.

Median – twenty-eight years old.

Mean – twenty-eight years and seven months old.

With or without the outliers, the median age of the killer women in this study is twenty-eight years old.

~

Number of children

(at the time of the murders)

Francine Hughes – four children.

Diane Downs – three children at the time of the shootings and then she got pregnant pending trial.

Betty Broderick – four children (five children - one deceased).

Susan Smith – two children.

Darlie Routier – three children.

Andrea Yates – five children.

Susan Wright – two children.

Darlene Gentry – three children.

Mary Winker – three children.

Jodi Arias – no children.

Shayna Hubers – no children.

Colleen McKernan – no children. (Her husband's son doesn't qualify considering the child did not want to have to spend time with her and her marriage to the child's father was very short-term).

Summary of Category Number Two

NUMBER OF CHILDREN

Mode – three children.

Median – three children.

Mean – 2.4 children.

If we study the number of children using just the women who had children then the results are as follows.

Mode – three children.

Median – three children.

Mean – 3.2 children.

Therefore, the average between the group of women who had children at the time of the murders and the group which also included those who didn't have children at the time of the murders is 2.8 children.

~

Whether the killer was a victim of childhood abuse

(including physical, sexual, and emotional abuse)

This is a tough category to research given the inherent secrecy that exists in families where abuse occurs. So, we can only discuss the possibilities of whether abuse occurred in the killers' childhood. I will rate each case from one which is unlikely that abuse occurred and ten which is that the evidence of childhood abuse is obvious.

Francine Hughes – While there is no claim made by Francine or by anyone in her family of abuse in her childhood, it is likely that her mother was subjected to the same sort of treatment that she endured both during and after her own marriage to Mickey Hughes. At one point, Francine did escape the relationship with her children and she stayed at her mother and father's home.

However, her parents did not encourage her to divorce her abusive husband nor did they treat her as if she and the children were welcome to stay for an extended period of time. Therefore, it appears that her husband's abuse toward her was something that her parents did not find objectionable. When he arrived at her parents' home and told her to get in the car, there were no supportive family members encouraging her to refuse to get into his car.

Therefore, on a scale of one to ten points with one being unlikely and ten being obvious, and considering the zeitgeist of the times where society did not think it was proper to meddle into a "family matter" even when abuse was obvious – I will rate Francine's case at ten points to include both physical and emotional abuse with no information specific to sexual abuse in her childhood.

Diane Downs – According to Diane Downs her father sexually molested her when she was a young teen girl. She said that her father took her for a ride in the country then stopped the car and reached over to fondle her breasts. It's interesting to note that when Diane Downs shot her children, she took them for a drive in the country then stopped her car and got her gun out of the trunk of her car. Perhaps there is some sort of deep sub-conscious connection to the powerlessness she felt as a child and the sense of power she exerted when she pulled the trigger. Could it be that in some twisted way the person she was shooting was her own father who had abused her when she was young?

I rate Diane Downs case at ten points.

Betty Broderick – Betty was born and raised in a strict Catholic home with parents who did not seem interested in hearing anything at all about how she suffered abuse in her marriage. The rules were clear – divorce would bring shame to her family and it was her job to make her parents proud of her, not to bring shame to the family name. Therefore, it appears that perhaps her parents accepted abuse and maltreatment as simply their daughter fulfilling her role as a dutiful wife and mother with her husband being the head of the household and the one in charge.

I rate Betty Broderick's case at eight points since I believe it is more likely than not that she was conditioned as a child to excuse maltreatment and abuse. I also believe that she was conditioned to perform for her parents, to succeed, regardless of the costs to her well-being.

Susan Smith – In Susan Smith's case she claimed that her step-father had been sexually abusing her from the time she was a teenager up to and including the months before she murdered her children. This is perhaps the most serious of any childhood sexual abuse cases I've ever heard of to learn that the sexual abuse and control was continuing long after the victim reached adulthood. Clearly, if her allegations are true, the inner rage she must have carried with her as an adult may have played a part in her actions the day she murdered her children.

Therefore, I rate Susan Smith's case at ten points.

Darlie Routier – According to Darlie, her step-father sexually molested her the first time when she was just eight years old. Her mother did not divorce Darlie's abusive step-father for another ten years, after Darlie had already become an adult. Just three weeks before Darlie murdered her children, she handed them over to the man she claimed had sexually molested her when she was young and allowed him to have her children spend the day with him while she celebrated Mother's Day without her children.

In Darlie's family of origin following the murders, her kid sister and her mother were involved in a physical altercation where one ended up with a bite mark on her thigh and one ended up with a bleeding lip. This leads me to believe that not only was Darlie raised in a home where she was subjected to sexual abuse, that she may have also been subjected to physical abuse.

Therefore, I rate Darlie Routier's case at 10 points.

Andrea Yates – It is unknown whether Andrea suffered from childhood sexual abuse. In her case, it appears that she suffered from mental illness which was exacerbated by post-partum psychosis. Her doctor advised Andrea to stop having children but she and her husband, Rusty Yates, ignored the doctor's advice and continued to have more children.

Without any claims made it is difficult to assess her case. However, based on the fact that Andrea was a follower not only of her husband even when he was off the rails with not putting the best interests of his family before his own desire to live in a bus and at one point in a camper, but also of a "minister" and his wife who seemed to be brainwashing her about the evils of the world, I think it is highly likely that Andrea had an overbearing parent who she tried her best to please.

Therefore, I rate Andrea's case as being more likely than not at 7 points.

Susan Wright – Susan's mother admitted that her husband was abusive toward her during the years they raised their daughters together. Susan's sister also admitted that abuse was rampant in their childhood home and that she was concerned for her sister's well-being in her own marriage because she was aware of the fact that her sister had married a man just like their father.

After watching documentaries on this case where Susan's sister speaks very directly about the abuses that occurred in her childhood, I rate her case at 10 points.

Darlene Gentry – There has been no claim of any childhood abuse in Darlene Gentry's life.

Therefore, I rate her case at one point for "unlikely".

Mary Winkler – There has been no claim of any childhood abuse in Mary Winkler's life. However, Mary's case is a bit different from Darlene Gentry's case in that Darlene was independent, successful, and active. Mary's actions of getting herself involved in the financial scam that ended up costing her many thousands of dollars combined with her fear of telling her husband about it leads me to believe that as a child she was conditioned to fear being punished and was not trained to think for herself.

Therefore, even without any claim of childhood abuse, I rate her case at eight points.

Jodi Arias – According to Jodi Arias she was abused as a child. However, if you pay close attention to her trial testimony it appears she is attempting to make the claim without any credible evidence or statements which would support her accusation against her parents, specifically her mother, for hitting her with a spatula.

Therefore, I rate her case at 3 points considering she is making the claim, but I find her claim to unlikely true or severe enough to be considered abuse.

Shayna Hubers – There has been no claim of any childhood abuse in Shayna Hubers' life. However, there did seem to be a highly unusual dependency on her mother based on her trial testimony. Before she shot her ex-boyfriend, Shayna called her mother in tears. Her mother hopped in the car and rushed to her side. And just one day later Shayna shot and killed her ex-boyfriend then failed to immediately dial 911. Instead, she called her mother and asked her what she should say to the police.

Therefore, based on what seems to be a relationship with her mother that appears to have blurred boundaries at best, I rate her case at eight points.

Colleen McKernan – There has been no claim of any childhood abuse in Colleen McKernan's life. However, due to what seemed to be an overpowering need to control all aspects of her and her husband's lives and her need to try to control her husband's son's life too, I think it's clear that she had issues which had yet to be resolved.

Therefore, I rate her case at seven points.

Summary of Category Number Three

WHETHER THE KILLER WAS A VICTIM OF CHILDHOOD ABUSE

Mode – 10 (Obvious)

Median – 8

Mean – 7.7

It's interesting to note that the two cases of KILLER WOMEN who did not seem to have suffered from being adult survivors of childhood abuse were Jodi Arias and Darlene Gentry. Both women used guns to kill the men they claimed to love. And both women staged the crime scene in an attempt to avoid prosecution. Both women were highly intelligent, articulate, and they both seemed to think they could tell their stories and easily fool the investigators.

While it is difficult overall to determine whether there was abuse in the childhoods of these KILLER WOMEN, overall it appears that it is highly likely that if a woman becomes a killer that she is likely suffering from some sort of unresolved rage stemming from her childhood.

I think the Darlie Routier case really stands out in this area – She handed her children over to her step-father, the man she claimed started sexually assaulting her when she was an eight-year-old little girl, just three weeks before the murders. ON MOTHER'S DAY, no less. There's something there. Something very intriguing. As if she was giving her own mother the gift of forgiving the man who her own mother evidently didn't protect her from.

Four weeks before the murders, Darlie was so depressed that she couldn't get out of bed, couldn't stop crying, and she started to write a suicide note in her journal addressed to her children hoping they would one day be able to forgive her for what she was about to do.

Was that the day she agreed to allow her childhood molester to take her own children for the day the following week?

Was she expected to say yes? Who arranged it? Whose idea was it in the first place for her to be expected to hand her children over to the man she says first molested her when she was a little girl?

Was she silenced when she was a child? And then silenced again when her family expected her to forgive and forget and act like nothing had happened? Her mother stayed married to the man she says molested her for another ten years. Could it be that Darlie was not believed? Could it be that handing her children over to the man who molested her was the beginning of the end?

According to expert Dr. Phillip Resnick, there are five specific categories of filicide – Altruistic (to end pain and suffering), Altruistic (to protect the child from the evil world), Unwanted child, Physical abuse that ends (not intentionally) in death, and Spousal revenge filicide. Up to this point I've always thought that Darlie Routier committed Spousal revenge filicide to deny her husband access to their children in a pending divorce. However, I've started to wonder if it may be possible that at some deep and very dark level if Darlie was actually committing Altruistic filicide (to protect her children from the evils of the world) after making the mistake of handing her children over to spend the day with the man she claims had molested her when she was a child.

Diane Downs' case is also one that could raise the same questions as Darlie's case does. Diane Downs insists that her father molested her when she was a young teen girl. Most people believe, including the prosecutor in her case, that Diane wanted to rid her life of her children so that her very married boyfriend who didn't want children might return to her. But what if they're wrong? Shortly before Diane Downs shot her children, she moved with her children to live in close proximity to her parents.

Before that she lived far away. But she accepted a job transfer to be near her parents and she worked right with her father at the post office where he was the postmaster and she was a postal worker with a mail route of her own.

Her children spent most of the time at their grandparents' home. She would often have dinner at her folks' house with her children. Could it be that at some very deep and dark level that Diane Downs was struggling with inner rage toward the man who had molested her yet she subjected her own children to being under his roof on a nearly daily basis?

Susan Smith is another example of the potential for evil acts if one is still suffering from the effects of childhood sexual abuse. In her case, she claimed that the abuse had never stopped. Could it actually be that when she murdered her children that it wasn't about her ex-boyfriend not wanting children but was instead her unresolved rage toward what seemed to her to be her powerful step-father who she claimed was continuing to take advantage of her?

Overall, the results are clear that KILLER WOMEN are highly likely to be adult survivors of childhood abuse.

~

Socioeconomic status

For this category, I will classify each woman into one of three groups. Group one will be if they were dependent on the state to feed their children. Group two will be if they were financially independent or in a marriage which allowed them to provide well for their children. And group three will be if they are wealthy.

Francine Hughes – Francine Hughes was attending secretarial school to help lift herself out of poverty, so she could provide for her children and herself without depending on welfare. Group one.

Diane Downs – Diane Downs had a good job with the post office which offered excellent pay and benefits. She may have been a bad mother but by all accounts she was a hard worker. Group two.

Betty Broderick – Betty Broderick lived in an affluent area, she had her college degree, and her ex-husband was court-ordered to pay her alimony in an amount higher than most people in the United States earn. While she had difficulty in actually collecting what he was ordered to pay her, the fact remains that financially speaking she was in group three.

Susan Smith – Susan Smith had a good job and a supportive ex-husband who was involved in her children's lives. Group two.

Darlie Routier – Darlie Routier's husband's business appeared to have been failing but he was resourceful and any difficulties with his business were likely short-term. Group two.

Andrea Yates – Andrea's husband had a good job and they had a nice home in a very nice area. Group two.

Susan Wright – Susan Wright had a hard-working husband and they had a nice home. Group two.

Darlene Gentry – Darlene Gentry had a career of her own as an R.N. and her husband was also a hard worker. Group two.

Mary Winkler – Mary Winkler's husband was a minister and they lived in the parsonage. They had a nice home, a decent income, and lived in a nice area. Group two.

Jodi Arias – Jodi Arias seemed to struggle to make ends meet and she was known to borrow money from past boyfriends, including the ex-boyfriend she killed. Group one.

Shayna Hubers – Shayna Hubers was a college student at the time she killed her ex-boyfriend. Group one.

Colleen McKernan – Colleen and her husband owned their own home and they both had good jobs. Group two.

Summary of Category Number Four

SOCIOECONOMIC STATUS

Mode – Group two – middle class.

Median – Group two – middle class.

Mean – 1.83 just shy of group two – middle class.

Back in the day before VAWA it was widely believed that domestic violence and child abuse occurred in only the poorest of homes. This stereotype is absolutely false. Domestic violence and child abuse knows no boundaries, including the socioeconomic status of the parties involved.

In every single one of the cases we are comparing, these women had nice homes, access to health care, and they did not suffer from any food insecurity. They had cars in every case except one, and she had access to public transportation. Many of them had college degrees and good careers. Those who chose to be a stay-at-home mom benefitted from the income of their husbands.

Conclusion – KILLER WOMEN are middle class women who live in nice homes and who have opportunities for both getting an education and a good job, as well as having access to health care and transportation.

For this category I will assign points for having a support system in place ranging from one to three points depending on the type of support that was available.

Francine Hughes – Francine Hughes did not seem to have a support system in place. How could she? Her abuser lived right next door with his parents and would keep an eye on her daily. She was not allowed to have friends over to her home or to go anywhere or do anything without facing punishment from him for trying to establish a life for herself free from his abuse.

However, Francine was definitely trying to make the best of the situation she was in. She reached out to social services for help. She called the police and asked for their help too even though they weren't able to get involved in what were deemed at the time to be a "family matter". She also signed up for classes with the hope that she would be able to get a job as a secretary and raise herself and her children out of poverty.

Clearly, it appears that Francine did not have help from her family, from her husband's family, or from any friends.

Points – one point for school, one point for social services, and one point for calling the police even though they weren't helping her. Three points.

Diane Downs – Diane Downs had a good job, a decent home, and her mother took care of her children for her on a daily basis. Three points.

Betty Broderick – Betty Broderick had a good job, a decent home, and she had a boyfriend who was loving and kind. Three points.

Susan Smith – Susan Smith had a good job, a decent home, and her ex-husband was involved with her children's lives. Three points.

Darlie Routier – Darlie did not have a job and she and her husband were late on their bills and sinking fast in the financial stresses associated with her husband's business. However, Darlie had hired help at home, she had her sister staying with her and friends and family members who visited her regularly, and she had a husband who took responsibility for supporting the family. Three points.

Andrea Yates – Andrea Yates had a husband who kept getting her pregnant even when the doctor told them not to have more children due to her health concerns. His mother would sometimes stay with her during the day while he worked. But I don't know if that was a plus or minus for Andrea. I think when it comes to what kind of support Andrea had I would have to say none. To me it just seems that when a husband has his wife and children living in a bus, or when he keeps right on getting her pregnant even when the doctor said not to, that instead of being any source of support for her that he was actually creating the problem or causing the problem to worsen. Zero points.

Susan Wright – Susan Wright had in-laws close by who helped with taking care of her children, she and her friends had a group of friends they enjoyed time with, and she had a sister and mother both who she was close to. Three points.

Darlene Gentry – Darlene Gentry had a nice family, a good job, and friends she could count on. Three points.

Mary Winkler – Mary Winkler had a large church family. However, with her husband being the minister it may have been very difficult for her to ever really reach out to any of the members of the church.

Therefore, it is possible that Mary felt she didn't really have anybody she could lean on or that she could confide in. Zero points.

Jodi Arias – Jodi Arias appeared to have family members who bent over backwards to be there for her. She was close to her parents, to her sister, and to her grandmother. She was able to also stay in contact with past boyfriends who were supportive of her. Three points.

Shayna Hubers – Shayna Hubers was a college student who was very close to her mother but did not appear to have a close-knit group of friends. I question her relationship with her mother as to whether it was supportive or not as in whether it was truly in her best interest. Zero points.

Colleen McKernan – Colleen McKernan had a neighbor who helped her, a mother-in-law who treated her well, and her husband's group of friends who also treated her well. She had a good job and she was also in the reserves so she had access to many people in her career to bond with and to lean on. Three points.

Summary of Category Number Five

WHETHER THE KILLER HAD ANY HELP AVAILABLE TO HER

Mode – Three points.

Median – Three points.

Mean – 2.4 points.

Back in the day before VAWA was passed in 1994, it was difficult for battered women to find any support or any help to escape an abusive relationship. When Francine Hughes killed her abuser, she had already tried many times to get help from the police. But they did not get involved. When her abuser hit a police officer that was a different story. They put him in cuffs and threw him in jail immediately. But when he hit Francine, nothing could be done to make him stop abusing her.

When Diane Downs shot her children there was little help available for children who were suffering at home with an abusive parent. Shortly before Diane Downs shot her children, one of her daughters told her grandmother's neighbor that she was afraid of her own mom. If that had happened today, that neighbor could have reported the family to CPS and a full investigation would have taken place. And it probably wouldn't have even taken a neighbor to get involved because by then the school or the pediatrician would have likely reported Diane Downs long before the child ever expressed fear of her mother to her grandmother's neighbor. So, in Diane's defense, there were not safeguards in place yet in our society which would have helped her to get the help she needed to be a better parent. And if not, then the children could have been removed from her home altogether when there were obvious warning signs of the way she mistreated them.

When Betty Broderick killed her abusive ex-husband there was no help available for a battered woman, especially when she lived in a nice home and drove an expensive car. Even the prosecutor in Betty's case claimed that she KNEW that Betty was not an abused woman BECAUSE SHE HAD MONEY.

So all three women suffered somewhat due to the fact that before VAWA there truly was not any help for women who were struggling with dealing with an abusive ex-husband or who clearly needed help in the parenting department.

But even though there wasn't help available on a macro level societal movement toward awareness and intervention, both Betty Broderick and Diane Downs did have the ability to begin a counseling relationship with someone trained in their area of need. They both had the means to pay for counseling. And they both owed it to their children to do so.

I can see how Betty Broderick did what she did. I can see how she felt she had no other choice at that moment but to commit suicide. To her, she was at the end of her journey. She simply couldn't take one more day of the abuse. But she did have the help she needed. If only she would have asked for it.

I will never be able to understand how Diane Downs did what she did though. Whatever her motive was, it's clear that she murdered her daughter and attempted to murder her other daughter and her son too. She should have been in counseling ever since her first marriage ended. And in counseling she could have perhaps formed a relationship of trust and known that someone cared about her well-being even if it seemed nobody else did. But most importantly, she could have received counseling to learn how to love herself just as she was instead of the way she seemed to believe that her core value was as a sexual being.

The KILLER WOMEN who killed their husbands or their ex-boyfriends after VAWA yet claimed they were battered women, I'm sorry but I don't buy it. With VAWA the police departments and the court system were obligated by law to respond for their call for help. So, I'm sorry, but I don't believe the battered woman syndrome should even be allowed to be used in court for cases post-VAWA.

As for child killers Darlie Routier, Susan Smith, and Andrea Yates, who all seemed to clearly be in need of mental health services, I wonder what impact the cuts to mental health services in the 1990s had on their cases. Is it possible that if the cuts had not taken place that these women would have gotten the help they seemed to so desperately need?

~

Education and employment options

In this category I will score points for education and employment. Zero is neither applies. Five is that one exists. And ten is that both existed.

Francine Hughes – Francine did not have a college degree. However, she was enrolled in a vocational program to learn secretarial skills so she would be able to get a good job and support her family. She was not working when she killed her ex-husband. Score – five points.

Diane Downs – Diane Downs had a good job with the post office where her dad was postmaster. Score – five points.

Betty Broderick – Betty was college educated and she had a new career at the time she killed her ex-husband. Score – ten points.

Susan Smith – Susan Smith had a good job. Score – five points.

Darlie Routier – Darlie did not have an education or a job when she killed her children. Score – zero points.

Andrea Yates – Andrea had a college degree and she held a good job as an R.N. before she killed her children. She chose to be a stay-at-home mom therefore her point score will be ten points.

Susan Wright – I believe that Susan Wright had a college degree or vocational training and a career working as a dental hygienist. Ten points.

Darlene Gentry – Darlene Gentry had both a college education and an excellent job as an R.N. Ten points.

Mary Winkler – Mary Winkler had a college education and she chose to be a stay at home mom. Ten points.

Jodi Arias – Jodi did not have a college degree and she did not have a good job. Zero points.

Shayna Hubers – Shayna was in college at the time she killed her ex-boyfriend. At age 21, it was premature for her to be expected to have a career already. Ten points.

Colleen McKernan – Colleen McKernan had a college degree and a good job. Ten points.

Summary of Category Number Six

EDUCATION AND EMPLOYMENT OPTIONS

Mode – 10

Median – 10

Mean – 7

Clearly, the KILLER WOMEN were well educated and had excellent job opportunities.

~

Stressors

In this category, points will be given for each stressor from the following list – financial, hormonal, physical, mental, emotional, marital, familial (extended family), sexual, spiritual.

Francine Hughes – Francine suffered financial stressors as a mom raising her children on welfare. Poverty is a very difficult situation for a mother of four to deal with. Good for her for attending her secretarial classes to try to better her life and the lives of her children. She also suffered from physical, mental, and emotional stressors given the fact that she was living in fear of being beaten by her ex-husband for many years straight. She suffered from marital stressors because even though she had already divorced her abuser, he still treated her as if he owned her. Francine suffered from familial stressors both from her own family which did not protect her and from her in-laws who lived right next door and did not stop their son from abusing her. Francine suffered from sexual abuse given the fact that her abusive ex-husband raped her. I can only guess but I think that it's likely that Francine suffered from spiritual stressors given the fact that she probably prayed for God to protect her and her children then felt forsaken by God every time her abusive ex-husband harmed her or their children.

Francine Hughes – eight points.

Diane Downs – Diane quite possibly suffered from emotional, mental, familial, and relational stressors. Specific to emotional, mental, and familial stressors I'm not sure that living near her parents was such a good idea after all if it's true that her father sexually molested her when she was young. The relational stress she suffered was due to the fact that her very married lover from back at the post office in Arizona she worked at before transferring to Oregon told her in no uncertain terms that he did not want to have children. So her dreams of him relocating to be with her in Oregon were shattered shortly before she shot her children.

Diane Downs – Four points.

Betty Broderick – Financial stressors – Betty lost everything in her divorce. Her ex-husband was a powerful and well-connected lawyer who basically screwed her royally. He was able to get the house sold without her presence in the courtroom or her signature on the closing docs. He locked up her furniture, linens, dishes, EVERYTHING she owned and refused to allow her to have any of it. He "loaned" his brother the proceeds of the house sale and was somehow able to convince the court that her fair share of the marital property was just thirty-thousand dollars. Clearly, Betty suffered from financial stressors. Hormonal – Betty was almost 42 years old and possibly entering menopause. She also suffered many miscarriages and the loss of one of her babies shortly after he was born. And she had four children who lived so Betty was basically pregnant on an annual basis for a decade or more. Mental, emotional, marital, familial (extended family) stessors – Betty suffered abuse on all levels including spiritually also considering her strict Catholic upbringing and her deeply held belief that marriage was a sacred bond not only with her ex-husband but also with God.

Betty Broderick – Seven points.

Susan Smith – Hormonal, mental, emotional, marital, familial (extended family), sexual, spiritual – If it's true that Susan's stepfather was still abusing her sexually then that certainly counts as a sexual stressor. She was also dealing with an ex-boyfriend who she believed dumped her suddenly because she had children. And her children were very young so it wasn't that long ago at the time of the murders that her body went through hormonal changes.

Susan Smith – Seven points.

Darlie Routier – financial, hormonal, physical, mental, emotional, marital, familial (extended family), sexual, spiritual. Darlie Routier suffered in every area included in this category except sexually and spiritually. At her trial, she testified that she was not someone to go to church. In all of her interviews she seems very at peace with her religious beliefs and practices. Financially - she and her husband were broke. Hormonal - she had just had a baby ten months before the murders and had just had her first monthly cycle four weeks before the murders since she got pregnant with the baby. She was exhausted yet unable to sleep which is a difficult physical stressor. Mental and emotional – her best friend begged Darlie to get the help she needed but she refused because she thought it wouldn't look good down the road in a custody battle. Marital – her husband's business was faltering, the bills weren't paid, his car needed repairs so he was using Darlie's car leaving her stranded at home with three sons to raise while her husband was out driving around with her kid sister instead of working at the shop. Yes, there was marital stress. Familial – I think handing her children over to the man who molested her when she was a child was more stressful for her than she realized at the time.

Darlie Routier – Seven points.

Andrea Yates –hormonal, physical, mental, emotional, marital, spiritual. Six points.

Susan Wright – physical, mental, emotional, marital – I believe that Susan Wright was being abused by her husband. Four points.

Darlene Gentry – zero points.

Mary Winkler – financial, mental, emotional, marital, sexual, spiritual. Six points.

Jodi Arias – financial, marital (or relational) sexual, spiritual. – Financially speaking it sounds like Jodi Arias has always struggled and has depended on borrowing money from others to get by so I do believe she had financial stressors. She had relational stressors at the time that she murdered her ex-boyfriend because she knew he was planning to go on vacation with someone new. I think she suffered sexually because she was used to having power over men with sex and her ex-boyfriend was not allowing her to maintain that control over him any longer. And I think that Jodi Arias also suffered spiritually because she was trying to convince her ex-boyfriend that she was a good Mormon girl who he would be able to marry but she knew that no matter what she tried to do to convince him that she was his spiritual mate that it would never work.

Jodi Arias – four points.

Shayna Hubers –mental, emotional, marital (relational), sexual - I think that Shayna was experiencing a very difficult time with her ex-boyfriend not wanting to be with her yet continuing to use her for sex. And I think it affected her emotionally and mentally too.

Shayna Hubers – four points.

Colleen McKernan – Colleen was such a control freak about money that there is little doubt she had plenty of financial stress going on when she killed her husband.

Marital and familial (extended family) stressors – I think that McKernan had a tough time convincing her husband that she was not to blame for the way his son didn't want to be anywhere near her. And I think she was having a tough time trying to keep her husband under her control so I think both areas of her life bothered her immensely. It sounds like her in-laws treated her well but I think she was probably having a tough time keeping up the façade of being a kind and good person who wasn't to blame for the troubles she and her husband were having.

Here is just one example of how McKernan operated. Before the wedding she had her husband call his mother and tell her that she was not invited to their wedding in order to keep costs down. And then right before the wedding he called and told her she could come. That's a little bit of insight into what Colleen McKernan is made of and just how conflict-averse Rob McKernan was too.

Colleen McKernan – Three points.

Summary of Category Number Seven

STRESSORS

Mode – 4

Median – 4

Mean – 4.2 stressors

There is no doubt that the KILLER WOMEN suffered from many stressors in their lives at the time they committed their crimes. However, it's interesting to note that the ones who appeared to be suffering the least were perhaps suffering from residual stressors from years past.

For example, on the surface it seems that Diane Downs had a good job and a great extended family. However, if it's true what she says about her dad molesting her, then obviously that changes everything.

The same is true for Shayna Hubers who did not seem to have any stressors really on the surface but then if you consider what being rejected sexually would feel like for a twenty-one-year old woman who seems to have an unnatural bond with her mother then perhaps the stressors she was really experiencing run deeper than what can be placed in this or that category.

Overall, it is difficult to measure stressors from the outside looking in. What one person may consider a stressor, another person may consider it a goal or a healthy challenge. Betty Broderick was probably devastated to not have access to what she believed would be hundreds of thousands of dollars of her own money. While Francine Hughes was probably thrilled to find out that the cost of her book would be covered by the state when she enrolled in her secretarial class.

Overall, these KILLER WOMEN did have too much stress going on in their lives at the time when they committed their crimes. And with stress unfortunately sometimes the sum total is much greater than all of it's parts, meaning that if you have one stressor and then you have another stressor on top of the first stressor, that the impact of having a second stressor piled on may seem as if there were three or four stressors piled on top.

In the interest of trying to learn what we can do as a society to help prevent tragedies like the ones in these cases, perhaps one of the best points to ponder would be how to help lower our stress levels so we're better able to cope with life as it happens without the risk of harming others.

~

Infidelity

In my research of these twelve cases I have found no allegations that the KILLER WOMEN were cheating on their spouses in both the cases involving domestic partner violence and the cases of filicide.

Summary of Category Number Eight

INFIDELITY

It's very interesting that in researching twelve random cases which occurred over a span of four decades that infidelity was not found in even one case. There were stressors in the relationships, to be sure. But infidelity was not one of them.

~

How the killer presented herself post incident

In this category, I will assign points in the following manner – if the KILLER WOMAN feigned innocence and took steps to cover up her crimes, I will assign her case ten points. If the KILLER WOMAN immediately took responsibility for her actions, I will assign her case one point. And if the KILLER WOMAN danced around with unbelievable accusations against her victim then I will assign points somewhere in between one and ten points.

Francine Hughes – one point. Francine Hughes told her children to get in the car then she lit the bed on fire where her abusive ex-husband was sleeping. She ran out of the house, hopped in the car, and drove directly to the police station and reported what she had done. She never hesitated to take full responsibility for her actions.

Diane Downs – ten points. Diane Downs drove to the emergency room and reported that a bushy-haired stranger had waved her down to carjack her car with her children in it. She claimed that he shot her children and that she scuffled with him and he shot her in the arm. Though her stories have seemed to change over the years, she has maintained her claim that a stranger shot her children and that she has been wrongfully convicted.

Betty Broderick – one point. Betty Broderick drove away from her abusive ex-husband's house but not in any attempt to hide what she had done. She got her affairs in order, called a lawyer, and turned herself in. She has admitted from day one that she shot him.

Susan Smith – seven points. At first, Susan Smith came up with an absurd story of a carjacking by a black male. However, the intersection where she said the carjacking took place did not have a red light unless there was more than one car present. So, the investigators were soon onto her and were able to get a confession just eight days after the incident occurred. Because she did confess fully in such a short time she does not qualify for the full ten points.

Darlie Routier – ten points. Twenty-two years after murdering her children, Darlie Routier still insists she is innocent. Fundraisers continue while she and her supporters claim that if only they can run more tests then surely she will be released from death row soon. She richly deserves ten points.

Andrea Yates – one point. Immediately after Andrea Yates drowned her five children in the bathtub in her home, she called her husband at work and told him that she needed him to come home. She has admitted her actions fully since day one.

Susan Wright – seven points. Susan Wright stabbed her husband 193 times, buried him in the backyard, and filed for a protection order against him. At first glance, her case appears to earn a ten-point ranking. However, in her case, I actually believe that she believed her husband might return. I think Susan Wright was abused by her husband. And I think he had such total power and control over her that even after he was dead that she lived in fear of him.

Darlene Gentry – ten points. Darlene Gentry staged the crime scene to try to fool the investigators into believing that an intruder had shot her husband and stolen his guns. Shortly after the murder, Darlene found property that was available for sale that had a pond on it. She told the builder that her husband, Keith, would have wanted his sons to have a nice pond right on their property so she agreed to purchase the property. Then she dumped the gun she used to kill her husband into the pond and called the builder and told him to go ahead and fill the pond in. The investigators set up surveillance at the property in question and had the builder call Darlene back and tell her that before they could fill the pond area in that they had to drain it.

Sure enough, Darlene showed up fast to try to find the gun which she had thrown into the pond before the builder would have had time to have the pond drained.

The investigators got it all on tape and arrested her. She definitely qualifies for ten points.

Mary Winkler – seven points. I don't think Mary Winkler deserves the full ten points. However, I also don't think she is as much of a victim as she presented herself to be at her trial. Just my opinion, but I think that the financial mess she had created shortly before she killed her husband had a lot to do with why she did what she did. Was she abused? I don't know. She said she was and the jurors believed her so I suppose, yes, she was. However, the sort of abuses she disclosed were far different than physical abuse or being trapped physically in a marriage with nowhere to turn for help.

Mary Winkler's husband, Matthew, was a well-respected minister. They lived in a nice home and were surrounded by a loving church family. Surely, Mary should have had resources available to her if in fact she was being abused at home. Her case was long after VAWA was passed in 1994. So her case is very different from Francine Hughes' case when the police did not care to get involved or Betty Broderick's case when society still hadn't learned that domestic violence occurs regardless of any socioeconomic status. So, I gave Mary Winkler a seven. She didn't go directly to the police station. She went to the beach with her children. However, when the police officers located her she did cooperate and admit her actions.

Jodi Arias – ten points. Jodi Arias not only attempted to stage the crime scene then ran off to her next prospect for a boyfriend's house in another state, but she also then interjected herself into the investigation as a caring friend who was interested in helping to find the killer. I have no idea how many different stories she told but there were many, ranging from saying she wasn't in Arizona to admitting she was there but insisting there were two people who killed Travis and who almost killed her two. Her most famous line perhaps was during the investigation when she said to mark her words that no jury would ever convict her.

Shayna Hubers – ten points. Shayna Hubers called her mother after murdering her ex-boyfriend to find out what to say to the police. In her interview she said that she gave her ex-boyfriend the nose job he always wanted. And she laughed. She also wondered out loud if other men may decide not to date her after what she had done. At her trial, she testified that her ex-boyfriend was abusive toward her and that she shot him in self-defense. But the jurors saw through her lies and sent her to prison for life.

Colleen McKernan – ten points. Colleen McKernan seems to have been a total control freak who demanded to have total control over her new husband too. If he wanted to get a hair cut he had to ask Colleen permission in order for her to give him the money from the envelope marked "hair cut". And if that money was gone, then no luck on the hair cut idea.

The night she killed her husband they were at a party and she glanced out the window and thought she saw her husband doing a line of coke. She evidently wasn't upset about the idea that he might be doing coke, which according to his friends, he was not doing. She was upset because then that would mean that he would have spent money from their transportation envelope, and the thought that he had already spent their transportation money for the week absolutely infuriated her.

She stormed outside to where he was sitting at the picnic table and proceeded to lambaste the man she claimed to love. Their friends asked them to leave and as he was walking with her to the car she screamed out that none of what had just happened was her fault.

I think when she killed him that he told her he was leaving her. And being the control freak that she seems to be, I think she decided right then and there that if he thought for one second that she was going to give up control of him that he was wrong.

Summary of Category Number Nine

HOW THE KILLER PRESENTED HERSELF POST INCIDENT

Scaled 1-10 with 1 being "admitted" and 10 being "denied"

Mode – 10

Median – 8.5

Mean – 7.0

Overall, specific to the twelve KILLER WOMEN in this study, they are likely to deny taking responsibility for their actions. There were just three women in all who impressed me as being ready to step right up to the plate immediately following the incident which certainly adds credibility to their stories. Francine Hughes who had already suffered for many years before she finally killed her abuser. Betty Broderick who also had already suffered for many years before she finally killed her abuser. And Andrea Yates who I think truly believed that she was saving her children from the evils of the world we live in (Altruistic filicide).

I believe that Francine Hughes was trapped with no way out. I believe when she killed her abuser that she was doing the only thing she knew how to do to protect her children and herself from having to suffer through another decade of torture.

I believe that Betty Broderick did not plan to commit murder when she shot her abuser. Her jurors also believe that she didn't plan to kill him since they found her guilty of second-degree murder, not first. Like Francine Hughes, I believe that Betty Broderick felt she was trapped too. But her escape plan was not to kill her abuser. Her plan was to kill herself. She said that if he refused to honor her final plea for him to leave her the hell alone then she intended to "splatter" her brains all over the walls of his new house so he would have to live with the memory of what he had caused her to do.

As if he would have cared.

And Andrea Yates also seems absolutely sincere in her claims that she was sending her children on to a better life (in heaven) and that it was her responsibility as their mother to protect them from the evils of this world.

But the others? By not owning up to their actions immediately then to me it seems they lose any credibility they may have otherwise had.

Short Summary of Results

Age – Twenty-eight years old.

Number of children – Three children.

Whether the killer was a victim of childhood abuse – Highly LIKELY.

Socioeconomic status – Middle class.

Whether the killer had any help available to her – Three or more sources of support.

Education and employment options – College-educated with job opportunities.

Stressors – Four or more stressors in major life impact categories such as marital stress, physical stress, financial stress, etc.

Infidelity – Zero incident rate of Killer Women committing adultery.

How the killer presented herself post incident - Scaled 1-10 with 1 being "admitted" and 10 being "denied"

Mode – 10

Median – 8.5

Mean – 7.0

pg. 54 KILLER WOMEN is an opinion essay written to compare and contrast the cases of women who kill their children, their husbands, or their ex-husband or boyfriend.

Conclusion

Hopefully, by comparing the cases of KILLER WOMEN we can learn something. My hope is that by examining the results and considering the similarities between these twelve cases that we can gain awareness which will help us recognize women in our lives who may need for us to reach out and help them.

None of these women who killed just suddenly one day decided to kill someone. There were warning signs. But society didn't know what to look for. So, each and every woman listed in this essay did not receive the help they needed.

Look at Francine Hughes – She called the police. She told her caseworker at social services what was happening. She told her parents. And her in-laws lived right next door and knew damn well that she and her children were in danger and living in constant fear of getting beat on.

Look at Diane Downs – Her first husband was abusive. Then one of the married guys at work used her then tossed her aside. If it was true that her father molested her then why didn't her mother and her other family members stand up for her? She had friends. She had lovers. She had co-workers. Why didn't somebody get involved in her life, and her children's lives, and offer to help?

Look at Betty Broderick – Look at how many years she suffered from being abused by her ex-husband! Why didn't any of their friends stand up and say YOU KNOW WHAT? THE WAY YOU ARE TREATING THE MOTHER OF YOUR CHILDREN IS INHUMANE! Why didn't the extended family members step up and tell him to knock it off?

Look at Susan Smith – She claimed that her stepfather was still molesting her as an adult. Why on earth didn't somebody see the signs and put a stop to it? Why on earth didn't she feel she could reach out for help? Her boyfriend at work? What do you think he was interested in? Taking advantage of the single mom who needed her job to support her kids. He knew she had kids when he was sleeping with her. Then he dumped her suddenly using her kids as his excuse for dumping her. Where was her support system? Were counselors available to her? Or was she going to just live her life bouncing from one man to the next hoping the next guy would treat her nice?

Look at Darlie Routier – IMO Darlie was as fake as it gets. Her implants, her hair, her nails, her southern belle accent that comes and goes depending on who she's talking to? Darlie was hurting. She was miserable. What did her friends do? Only one of them kept begging her to get the help she needed. The others said HEY LET'S GO ON VACATION! Shame on her husband and her family members who didn't help her get the help she needed. Instead, her husband said they talked about her suicidal thoughts and he got mad at her for how she was feeling and they never discussed it again. And four weeks later two of her children were dead.

Look at Andrea Yates – She and her husband at one point lived in a bus with their children!!! They were not poor. Her husband had a good job and she was an R.N. They had plenty of money to live in a house. Where was her family? Where were her friends? And after her doctor told her not to keep having babies, what did they do? They kept having babies!!!

Look at Susan Wright – Her in-laws lived right next door. Did they not know how their son was treating her and their grandchildren? She had a sister who is a psychologist!!!! She had a mother who cared!!! How on earth did it ever get to the point where she stabbed her husband 193 times and buried him in the backyard without anybody in her life realizing that she was waaaaay over the edge??? And if the abuse was known to her friends and family members, then why was she still married to him???

Look at Darlene Gentry – Nice home, successful career woman, great husband, beautiful kids. So why exactly did she kill her husband?

Look at Mary Winkler – She was surrounded by her church family. Why on earth didn't anyone in her church family care enough about the preacher's wife to notice she was miserable? She was alone? She was isolated? Where were her friends when she got messed up with the financial scam? Did she have anybody in her life she could confide in?

Look at Jodi Arias – Why on earth didn't anybody in her family help her get the help she needed? Were they afraid of her? Were they afraid to ever confront her? Did anybody ever get the idea that driving from California to Arizona to have sex with an ex-boyfriend wasn't a good idea?

Look at Shayna Hubers – I'm not blaming her victim's parents at all but there is something about her case that is bothersome. In the news it says that the night before the murder that she was a guest of her victim at his parents' home. So, how is it exactly that he was someone who she wouldn't leave alone? She was twenty-one years old. A kid. A college kid. She was way too young for a 29-year-old man to be using for sex and then expecting her to disappear. She had issues, to be sure. But being used by a much older man for sex certainly did nothing to help her. Where was her family? Where were her friends? Why didn't someone take her aside and fill her in that she was being used?

Look at Colleen McKernan – This case is troubling because I think her
strange behavior was evident from the start. She had her husband call
his mother and tell her to cut costs at their wedding reception they
were cutting her off the guest list. Then a few days before the
wedding they called again and said she could attend. Why on earth
didn't her husband call the entire wedding off right then and there?
And when his son cried about having to be alone with her? That's the
best warning sign right there! So why on earth didn't her new husband
get the heck away from her as fast as he could?

~

Take a look at the results. Age 28. The youngest was 21. The oldest was almost 42 years old. But eight out of twelve of these KILLER WOMEN were between the ages of 26 and 33 with the majority of them being 28 years old.

Number of children – Three. One of the KILLER WOMEN had five children. Most of them had three children. Yet, three of them didn't even have any children of their own.

Whether the killer was a victim of childhood abuse – Highly LIKELY. Every single one of the KILLER WOMEN we looked at in this study was an adult survivor of childhood abuse including either emotional, physical, or sexual abuse. In a few of the cases there is no report of any abuse however other signs tend to show that in fact there actually was. Most telling is that these women were not able to turn to their family of origin for help. Worst of all, in a couple of the cases, Darlie Routier and Diane Downs, they were expected by their families to hand their children over to the men they accused of sexually molesting them when they were chidren themselves.

Socioeconomic status – Middle class. Domestic violence, child abuse, and homicide, filicide, and whatever post-partum or hormonal issues that might be going on KNOWS NO SOCIOECONOMIC BOUNDARIES!

Whether the killer had any help available to her – Three or more sources of support. Each one of the KILLER WOMEN in this study had help available to them. Francine Hughes had the least amount of help and still she persevered and continued to reach out for help at every opportunity. If Francine Hughes can take public transportation to sign up for a secretarial class, then every woman can follow her example and do whatever they can to better their lives and the lives of their children.

Education and employment options – College-educated with job opportunities. The majority of the KILLER WOMEN in this study were well-educated and had excellent job opportunities available to them. Again, THERE IS NO SOCIOECONOMIC BOUNDARY to abuse.

Stressors – Four or more stressors in major life impact categories such as marital stress, physical stress, financial stress, etc. This is a very important category to consider in that every one of the KILLER WOMEN in this study had major life stressors going on at the time of the killings. This is so important for us to learn from. Stressors are real. And there is an effect of piling on one stressor on top of other stressors that exacerbates the effects of the stressors compared to if they were faced alone. For example, your neighbor is experiencing financial difficulties. Okay, so who isn't, right? But then her husband left her. Well, big deal. Divorce is happening everywhere, right? But then she is diagnosed with Lupus. And suddenly, she can't handle any of it anymore. Perhaps she could deal with any one of those stressors just fine on their own. But all three at once?

Infidelity – Zero incident rate of Killer Women committing adultery.

How the killer presented herself post incident - Scaled 1-10 with 1 being "admitted" and 10 being "denied"

Mode – 10

Median – 8.5

Mean – 7.0

This is a sign of the times we're living in I'm afraid when so many people just deny responsibility for their actions and look for any excuse they can find to pretend away their actions.

Like Colleen McKernan said when their friends asked her and her husband to leave the New Year's Eve party because she was screaming at her husband – NONE OF THIS IS MY FAULT!

~

What We Can Do to Help Other Women Before Its Too Late

Reach out to anyone you know who you feel may be at risk of harming themselves or others. Get involved. Learn. Research. Get training. Butt into their lives. You may be the only person brave enough to butt in and care.

Look at your co-workers. Look at your friends. Look at your family members. Is there anyone in your life right now who is struggling to cope with major stressors going on in their lives? Can you reach out to them and help them? Can you at least spend time talking with them and listening and maybe help them connect with services or other support people who can help them? Don't miss your chance to help someone in your life know that you care, that you're available if they need anything, and that you are willing to help them.

And finally, look at yourself – take a good hard look at your own life. Are you facing major stressors? Are you yelling at your children to "get the hell out of the house!" like Darlie Routier was? Are you chasing after a man to love you like Arias, Hubers, and Downs were before they turned violent?

Are you miserable in your marriage? Is your husband beating on you and your children? If so, there is help available for you to safely escape your abusive marriage.

Jump right into your friends lives and let them know you care. Take a good look at your own life and take healthy steps to improve your life and your children's lives like Francine Hughes did when she signed up for classes.

Give the help you can give. And get the help you need. Because you and your children deserve to be safe in your own home.

And you, and your children, deserve to be happy.

 KILLER WOMEN is an opinion essay written to compare and contrast the cases of women who kill their children, their husbands, or their ex-husband or boyfriend.

About the Author

Brenda Irish Heintzelman, BA, JD is an avid writer and speaker on the issues of family violence and child abuse. Brenda is the owner of mimediator.com and serves as a mediator and arbitrator specializing in domestic relations including custody, access, and child protection.

If you enjoyed this essay on the case of accused killer Christopher Watts please check out Brenda's other true-crime essays which are available on both kindle and amazon.com.

Unbelievable (Darlie Routier)

Confession (Darlie Routier)

The Whole Truth (Darlie Routier)

Haters (Christopher Watts)

Haters (Steven Avery)

Scapegoat (Terri Horman)

The Lie (Colleen McKernon)

Above the Law (Curtis Reeves)

Sacred Bond (Sabrina Limon)

Permission to Scream (Betty Broderick)

Scapegoat (Jodi Arias)

Scapegoat (Mary Winkler)

May 19, 1983 (Diane Downs)

Preview of

PERMISSION TO SCREAM

The Psychosocial Abuse of Convicted Husband Killer Betty Broderick

copyrighted material 2018

Brenda Irish Heintzelman

Early in the morning on November 5, 1989 Betty Broderick shot and killed her abusive ex-husband, Daniel Broderick, III. She didn't intend to hurt him. She intended to kill herself right in front of him if he refused to listen to her final plea to just leave her the hell alone.

He was a powerful well-connected lawyer who tortured Betty long after their separation with incessant court filings claiming she was mentally unstable. He wouldn't let up. And Betty couldn't take it anymore. If he refused to listen to her then her only escape was to commit suicide.

When Betty had taken just two steps into his bedroom he saw her and lunged for the phone. His sudden movement scared Betty and before she knew what was happening "the gun just went off".

Five times.

Betty Broderick was a battered woman long before the syndrome became widely known. She was beaten down for nearly twenty years straight as her husband physically, sexually, emotionally, spiritually, financially, and psychologically abused her.

Betty was stuck in the freeze response survival instinct. She didn't
know how to protect and defend herself from his abuse. And in 1989
she didn't have any help.

He robbed Betty of all she held dear – her children, her home, her
reputation for being a good mother, her marriage, her fair share of the
marital assets, and even her china and linens too.

In front of their children he called Betty a "monster" and "the beast".

While feigning concern for his safety, he taunted Betty then acted
shocked when she reacted in anger.

He told people she was crazy and would soon take her own life.

He continued to push and prod Betty until finally she decided to give
him what he wanted ~ her life.

But then just seconds before she planned to pull the trigger,

suddenly the gun was pointed at her abuser,

instead of herself.

Because sometimes,

battered women fight back.

~